FORTNITE:
Creative Mode

MEMORY USED

22,378 | 100,000

CHERRY LAKE PUBLISHING • **ANN ARBOR, MICHIGAN**

by **Josh Gregory**

CHERRY LAKE PRESS

Published in the United States of America by Cherry Lake Publishing
Ann Arbor, Michigan
www.cherrylakepublishing.com

Reading Adviser: Marla Conn MS, Ed., Literacy specialist, Read-Ability, Inc.

Library of Congress Cataloging-in-Publication Data
Names: Gregory, Josh, author.
Title: Fortnite : creative mode / by Josh Gregory.
Identifiers: LCCN 2019024708 | ISBN 9781534159631 (library binding) | ISBN
    9781534161931 (paperback) | ISBN 9781534160781 (pdf) | ISBN
    9781534163089 (ebook)
Subjects: LCSH: Fortnite Battle Royale (Game)—Juvenile literature.
Classification: LCC GV1469.35.F67 G7445 2020 | DDC 794.8—dc23
LC record available at https://lccn.loc.gov/2019024708

Cherry Lake Publishing would like to acknowledge the work of the Partnership
for 21st Century Learning, a Network of Battelle for Kids. Please visit
http://www.battelleforkids.org/networks/p21 for more information.

Printed in the United States of America
Corporate Graphics

Contents

Chapter 1

Your Very Own Island

I f you've played *Fortnite* before, you know that creativity is a big part of the game. Players get to customize their characters' looks and show off their unique creations to their friends. They also spend a lot

The world of *Fortnite* is packed with colorful, creative environments.

Building your own structures is a big part of the fun of *Fortnite*.

of time building forts and other structures as they play. But while creativity is important in the action-packed Save the World and Battle Royale modes of *Fortnite*, it is not the main goal. Players must instead focus their attention on defending themselves and defeating enemies. But what if they just want to relax and enjoy the more constructive parts of the game?

As *Fortnite*'s popularity grew, many players began asking for a more relaxed mode where they could experiment with the game's building system. In late 2018, *Fortnite*'s **developers** responded by adding a major new update called Creative mode to the game. Creative mode is exactly what it sounds like: a mode that lets players focus on building and creating within the wacky world of *Fortnite*. In Creative mode, you can take all the time you need to perfect your buildings. You don't have to worry about surprise attacks from enemies. You also get unlimited building materials. You even get access to special building tools that aren't available in the game's other modes.

Creative mode lets players build levels that are unlike anything on the main *Fortnite* island.

Some of the coolest things players make in Creative mode get added to the main Battle Royale island.

This means Creative mode will allow you to build the *Fortnite* world you've always dreamed of. You get an entire island to design and customize exactly how you want. You can build castles, pyramids, military bases, and much more. You could build a bunch of buildings to make your own city. Or, you could create one huge building with many floors, exits, and hidden rooms. It's all up to you.

Have you ever wanted to design your own video games? In Creative mode, you can experiment with making your own *Fortnite* game modes. You can adjust the rules and settings of the game world to make your own competitive mode with unique goals. Then you can invite your friends to try it out. You can decide where different weapons and other loot will show up, or whether there will be any vehicles on the map. Or you can simply build a fun location for your friends to explore.

If you create something really cool, it might even get chosen to become part of the main *Fortnite* Battle

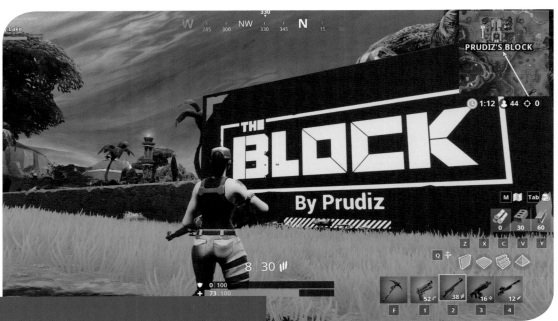

Players whose creations are added to the main island get their names displayed on a huge sign.

Careers in Game Design

If you enjoy creating new levels and game modes for your friends to play in Creative mode, you might have a future as a professional game developer. Game developers usually work together in teams. It can take hundreds of people to make a big blockbuster game. On the other hand, a smaller **indie** game can be created by just a handful of people. Some games are even created by lone developers who do everything themselves.

Each person on a development team usually specializes in one type of work. For example, some people focus on designing levels. Others create 3D graphics or write **code**. Musicians, actors, writers, and many others can all play important roles in creating games too. No matter what you're good at, there is probably a place for you in the world of video games.

Royale island. Then millions of other players around the world could explore your creation!

Creative mode is free for all *Fortnite* players to enjoy. To get started, all you need to do is select it from the main menu that appears when you load up *Fortnite* on your game console, computer, or mobile device. When you first start playing this mode, you might be overwhelmed with all the options. But once you dig in and start building, you'll become a master in no time. Let's get started!

Chapter 2

Getting Started

When you first load up Creative mode, you'll see a lobby screen much like the one in Battle Royale. Select the "Play" option to reach the server selection screen. Be sure "Start a Server" is highlighted, then hit the "Launch" button.

After the game finishes loading, you'll find yourself atop an island temple. This area is called the

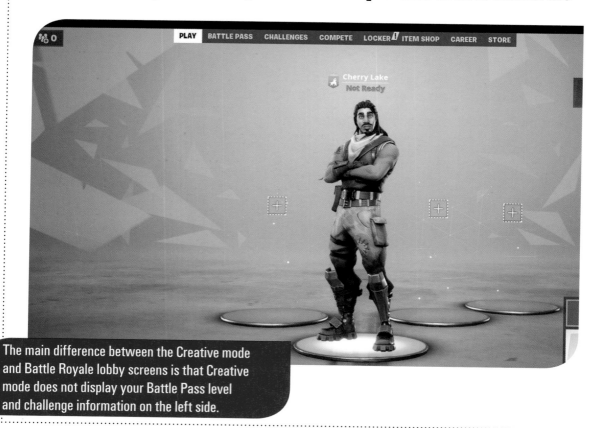

The main difference between the Creative mode and Battle Royale lobby screens is that Creative mode does not display your Battle Pass level and challenge information on the left side.

ISLAND 3
CREATED BY: Cherry Lake 0/1
E CHANGE ISLAND
3:53:27

If you press the button to "change island," you can choose from a variety of types of islands to build on, such as an arctic island or a volcanic island.

hub. In front of you will be five rift portals. The center portal will lead to your new Creative mode island. The other four lead to Creative mode islands that were built by other players. These are featured creations. You'll see different ones as you come back to the hub at different times. Feel free to try them out if you want to get a look at the cool things other players have created.

To get started with your own creations, simply walk into the center portal in the hub. You'll immediately find your character dropping from the sky as if you had leapt from the Battle Bus in a Battle Royale match. The island below you is much smaller than the main Battle Royale island. It is also mostly empty. This is good, because you'll need plenty of space to start building things!

Land wherever you like. Take a look around. This is the **default** island for Creative mode. Most of the area is flat, green space. There are some tall mountains on the north side of the island, and a small wooden shack

Your Creative mode island gives you plenty of room to build anything you can imagine.

toward the south end. If you want to go back to the hub, you can either select "Back to Hub" from the main menu or head to the portal on the central south edge of the island. From the hub, you can select the rift portal and choose to change its destination. Here, you can choose between several different types of islands, including an icy arctic setting and a tropical beach island. Feel free to choose whichever one you like best.

In Creative mode, you'll notice a few things on your screen that are a little different from other modes. First, there are small infinity signs where the numbers showing your building materials would be. This is because you don't need to gather materials in Creative mode. You have unlimited wood, stone, and metal to play with. You'll also notice instructions on the left side telling you how to fly. You can take flight and zoom around the island at any time in Creative mode by double-tapping the jump button. Hold the jump button to rise higher or the crouch button to drop down. To stop flying, double-tap the jump button again. Flying makes it easier to build big structures without needing to climb and run around them the long way. You'll be flying a lot in Creative mode, so play around and get used to the controls.

Touring the *Fortnite* Island

When you first load into the Creative mode hub, turn around and look behind you. On another level of the temple, you'll see a parked Battle Bus and several other portals. The portals are labeled with the names of locations that will be familiar to Battle Royale players, such as Pleasant Park and Dusty Divot. Going through one of these will drop your character onto the main *Fortnite* Battle Royale island at the location that is labeled.

On the island, you'll be able to discover loot, gather resources, and build like you normally would in Battle Royale. You won't have access to the special Creative mode building tools. But you can wander around and explore the island all you like. There will be no other players to interrupt you. This is a great way to learn the ins and outs of the island without any pressure. You might even spot details you never noticed in a fast-paced Battle Royale match.

You also have the option to let your character "phase" through objects while flying. This option is off by default. When you start flying, you will see an option on the side of the screen to turn phasing on. Once you do this, you can move right through walls, floors, and other objects. This really comes in handy if you want to build a complicated maze or a big building with lots of floors and rooms. While building, you can simply phase around so you don't have to run through your creation every time you want to adjust something. You can turn off phasing manually, or it will turn off automatically when you stop flying.

Look at the bottom-right corner of your screen, where your **inventory** spaces are. Next to your mining tool, you will see an icon for a smartphone. This item is only available in Creative mode. Like your mining tool, you always have it, and you can't drop it. But what can you do with a smartphone in *Fortnite*? Text some friends? Check your social media feeds? Actually, Creative mode's phone isn't really much of a phone at all. Instead, it is a powerful device that helps you build. To see how it works, equip it from your inventory. Then, point it at a tree. The tree will be highlighted in blue, and you should see a whole bunch of options appear on the left side of the screen. Press the button labeled "delete." The tree will suddenly disappear. That was a lot faster than hitting it with your mining tool!

Play around with the different options on the phone. Make copies of trees and rocks. Move them around. Place them in strange places and rotate them. You'll be using the phone almost constantly in Creative mode, so it pays off to experiment and learn the controls. Once you feel comfortable, you can start building your first structures!

Chapter 3

Building Up

You have a few options when it comes to building in Creative mode. First, you can do it the old-fashioned way. Just like in Battle Royale or Save the World, you can build walls, floors, roofs, and stairs. You can place them wherever you like, and they will snap together to form larger structures. The controls for placing and rotating these building pieces are

When you select building pieces using the phone, they will be highlighted in green.

the same as they are in the other modes. The biggest difference is that you have unlimited wood, stone, and metal to work with.

Remember that you can edit the shape of any building piece you place. For example, you can remove the center square and the one below it to make a door. Remove the top two rows of a wall to make a low wall. There are plenty of options for creating unique shapes, so play around. Again, these are all the same as they are in the other modes. If you're already a master builder in Battle Royale, those same skills will apply here.

Try building a simple tower. Now pull out your phone. Highlight all the pieces of your tower one by one and press the button labeled "Select" on each one. You can select up to 20 pieces at a time. Once the whole thing is selected, press the button labeled "Copy." Move to a nearby location, then press the button labeled "Paste." You will instantly build an exact copy of your tower. In fact, you can build all the towers you want now. You can even stack them on top of each other. You can copy and paste anything you build, as long as there is room. This will allow you to build very quickly once you get the hang of it.

Of course, Creative mode lets you do a lot more than just build normal *Fortnite* structures. Try opening your inventory. You will probably notice right away that it doesn't look like the inventory in other modes. At the top of the screen are tabs labeled **Prefabs**, Galleries, Devices, Weapons, Consumables, and Chest. Each one contains a range of special building materials and other items you can use to construct your island.

Prefabs are pre-built structures that you can drop onto your island. For example, there are log cabins,

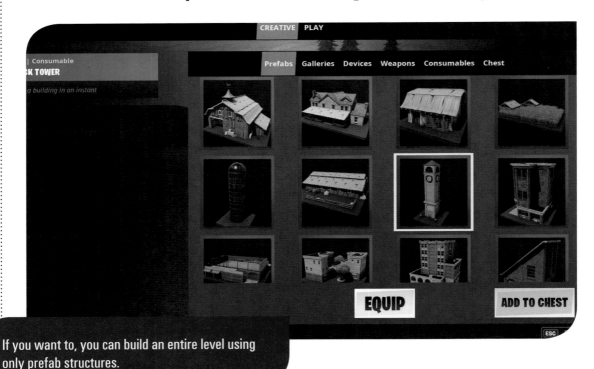

If you want to, you can build an entire level using only prefab structures.

Memory Management

As you start building, you might notice the slowly-filling bar beneath your health and shield bars at the bottom-center of the screen. It is labeled "Memory Used." As you build things on your island, this bar will slowly fill up. Everything you build takes up a certain amount of memory. Once the bar fills all the way up, you can't build anymore until you delete part of your creation. Don't worry, though. It takes a very long time to fill the memory bar all the way. If you do find yourself running out of space, take a close look at your creation and decide which parts can be removed. Another thing to remember is that multiple copies of the same structure will take up less memory than a bunch of unique pieces. So, for example, using several copies of the same log cabin from the prefab menu will take up less memory than using a lot of different log cabins.

snow-covered houses, and even a pirate ship. Scroll through and find one you like. Then choose to equip it. Leave your inventory screen, and you will see the prefab item in one of the slots in the bottom-right of the screen. Select it and you can toss it out in front of your character much like a grenade. When it lands, the prefab structure will suddenly pop up on your map.

Once the prefab structure is built, you can use your phone to adjust its details. For example, if you build a prefab house, you could remove a few walls.

Try moving around the furniture inside. Add on and make the house bigger by copying and pasting parts of it. Or simply delete the whole thing if you change your mind. It's all up to you.

Open your inventory screen again and check out the Galleries tab. Galleries work a lot like prefabs. You can choose one, add it to your inventory, and drop it onto your island. But instead of pre-made buildings, galleries are collections of objects you can build with. They are grouped together by themes. For example, there is a gallery full of rocks and another with various cars and other vehicles. Some have ramps for vehicles or special walls you can use to build better-looking buildings. Pick a gallery and equip it, then exit the inventory screen. Toss it onto your island and watch what happens.

You should see a bunch of objects scattered on the ground in front of you. Now you can use your phone to grab these objects, copy them, and move them around. You can combine them just like regular building pieces to create large structures. Throw down a few different galleries and combine the pieces in different ways. Think of them like the **palette** an artist

This gallery is filled with different cars you can use to decorate a level.

uses to mix colors for a painting. Once you are done with a gallery, you can use the phone to delete any stray pieces that are lying around.

Now try the Devices tab. This one contains all kinds of interactive objects you can place in your world. For example, there is a pinball bumper that will send players flying when they hit it. There are pads that make vehicles speed up. There are also pads that players can use to spawn different vehicles on your island.

Many of the items in the Devices tab can be customized after you place them. Simply walk up to one and press the button when you are prompted. You will then see a menu of options. Each device will have different ones. For example, a pinball bumper will let you choose how far players should bounce back when they hit it. It will also let you choose whether players should be damaged when they get knocked back. By combining the different devices and adjusting their options in creative ways, you can set up all kinds of

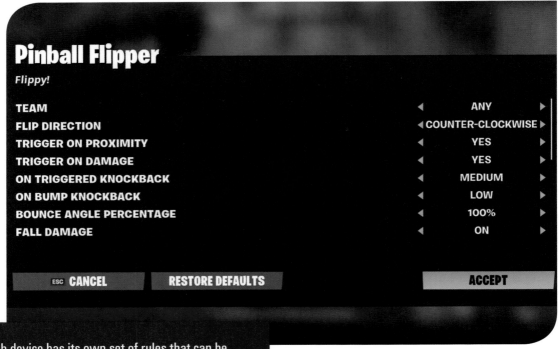

Pinball Flipper
Flippy!

TEAM	◄ ANY ►
FLIP DIRECTION	◄ COUNTER-CLOCKWISE ►
TRIGGER ON PROXIMITY	◄ YES ►
TRIGGER ON DAMAGE	◄ YES ►
ON TRIGGERED KNOCKBACK	◄ MEDIUM ►
ON BUMP KNOCKBACK	◄ LOW ►
BOUNCE ANGLE PERCENTAGE	◄ 100% ►
FALL DAMAGE	◄ ON ►

ESC **CANCEL**   **RESTORE DEFAULTS**   **ACCEPT**

Each device has its own set of rules that can be edited.

fun situations. For example, build a racetrack on your island, complete with ramps and speed-increasing pads. Then add some vehicles and try it out!

The Weapons tab in your inventory contains exactly what it says: all of the many weapons available in *Fortnite*. The Consumables tab is where you'll find ammo, health items, and all the other gadgets you can pick up while playing Battle Royale. You can add weapons and consumables to a treasure chest or Supply Llama, then place it somewhere on your island for players to find. Choose the items you want, then

You can fill up your very own Supply Llama with anything you want.

press the "Add to Chest" button. Now select the Chest tab. Choose "Create Llama" or "Create Chest" and the treasure will drop on the ground where your character is standing. Leave the inventory screen. Now you can use the phone to move the chest, make copies of it, or get rid of it.

The last main thing you need to learn about is the My Island menu. Open it up from the main menu and you will see all kinds of options for customizing your island. Some options can adjust the rules of the game when players visit your island. For example, you can make it easier to destroy objects with a mining tool or allow players to jump extra-high. You can also set up conditions for how players win or lose when playing on your island. There are a lot of options here, and you can use them to create very complex situations for players to solve.

As you build in Creative mode, you will see a message pop up from time to time to let you know that the game is saving your progress. Your work will also be saved automatically any time you quit the game, so don't be afraid of losing your creations.

Chapter 4

Sharing Your Creations

By now, you should have a good handle on how to build things and set rules for playing on your island. You may even have created something really cool already. Or maybe you want to try out some islands that were created by other players.

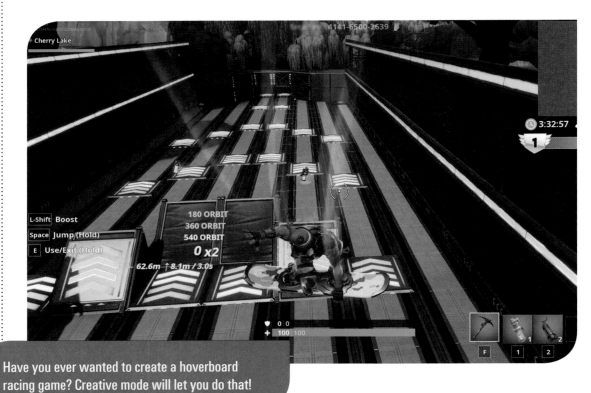

Have you ever wanted to create a hoverboard racing game? Creative mode will let you do that!

Inspiration Everywhere

Are you all out of ideas for things to build in Creative mode? Try looking outside the game for inspiration. Play other video games and think about the ways the developers planned out their levels and game modes. What works, and what doesn't? Are there any ideas you could apply to your Creative mode projects?

Go online or check out some books to see photos of incredible things people have built in real life, such as towering stone castles or enormous bridges. Try re-creating these in *Fortnite*. Or just use the bits and pieces you like best. Combine them however you want to!

Take a walk and observe your surroundings. As you watch movies or TV shows, think about things you can create. Keep a small notebook with you all the time and sketch out ideas as they pop into your head. You never know when you'll be inspired!

Creative mode players can share their work with others using special codes. They generate these 12-digit codes through the game menu in Creative mode, then share them on social media. Other players enter the codes in their game. Then they can explore the new island. Right now, not all players have the ability to create codes and share their work. As the developers at Epic Games continue to work on improving *Fortnite*, they are only allowing well-known, popular players to share their Creative mode levels. However, they plan to eventually give all players access to this feature, so keep building!

If you want to try out a player-made island, head to the hub. Check out the featured portals placed around the one leading to your island. Each one is already set to visit a player-made island that was chosen by Epic Games. You can also change each portal to lead to any player-created island you want. To do this, select the island and choose to enter a code. You will need the code of the island you want to visit. Once you enter it, you can enter a portal to the new island. The new portal will be saved, so you can go back to it any time.

One of the most exciting aspects of Creative mode is the possibility of having your level added to the main Battle Royale island. The Battle Royale island has an area called the Block. The developers at Epic Games choose the very best player-made levels from Creative mode and place them in the Block for all Battle Royale players to enjoy. There is no official way to submit levels to Epic Games for placement in the Block. Instead, the developers keep an eye on social media, message boards, and other places where

Check out the featured portals in your hub to see all the cool things other players have made in Creative mode. You might get a few ideas for things to build yourself.

players might share codes. They look for levels that show off the features of Creative mode in new and interesting ways.

Are you ready to become a master game designer? Creative mode gives you all the tools you need to get started. The rest is all up to you and your creativity, so get out there and build the *Fortnite* game mode you've always dreamed of!

Glossary

code (KODE) instructions written in a computer programming language

default (dih-FAWLT) the initial option selected in a game or other computer program before it is adjusted by a user

developers (dih-VEL-uh-purz) people who make video games or other computer programs

indie (IN-dee) game developers who operate independently instead of working for a big company

inventory (IN-vuhn-toh-ree) a list of the items your character is carrying

palette (PAL-it) a flat surface used for mixing colors of paint

prefabs (PREE-fabs) pre-built structures

Find Out More

BOOKS

Cunningham, Kevin. *Video Game Designer*. Ann Arbor,
Michigan: Cherry Lake Publishing, 2016.

Powell, Marie. *Asking Questions About Video Games*. Ann Arbor,
Michigan: Cherry Lake Publishing, 2016.

WEBSITES

Epic Games—Fortnite
www.epicgames.com/fortnite/en-US/home
Check out the official *Fortnite* website.

Fortnite Wiki
https://fortnite.gamepedia.com/Fortnite_Wiki
This fan-made website offers up-to-date information on the
latest additions to *Fortnite*.

Index

About the Author

Josh Gregory is the author of more than 150 books for kids. He has written about everything from animals to technology to history. A graduate of the University of Missouri–Columbia, he currently lives in Chicago, Illinois.